Nurse Swear

Vulgar Word Coloring Book for Ranting & Relaxing

By

S.B. Nozaz

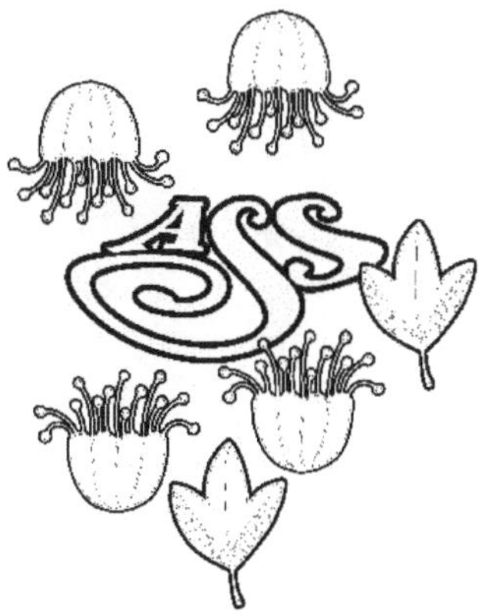

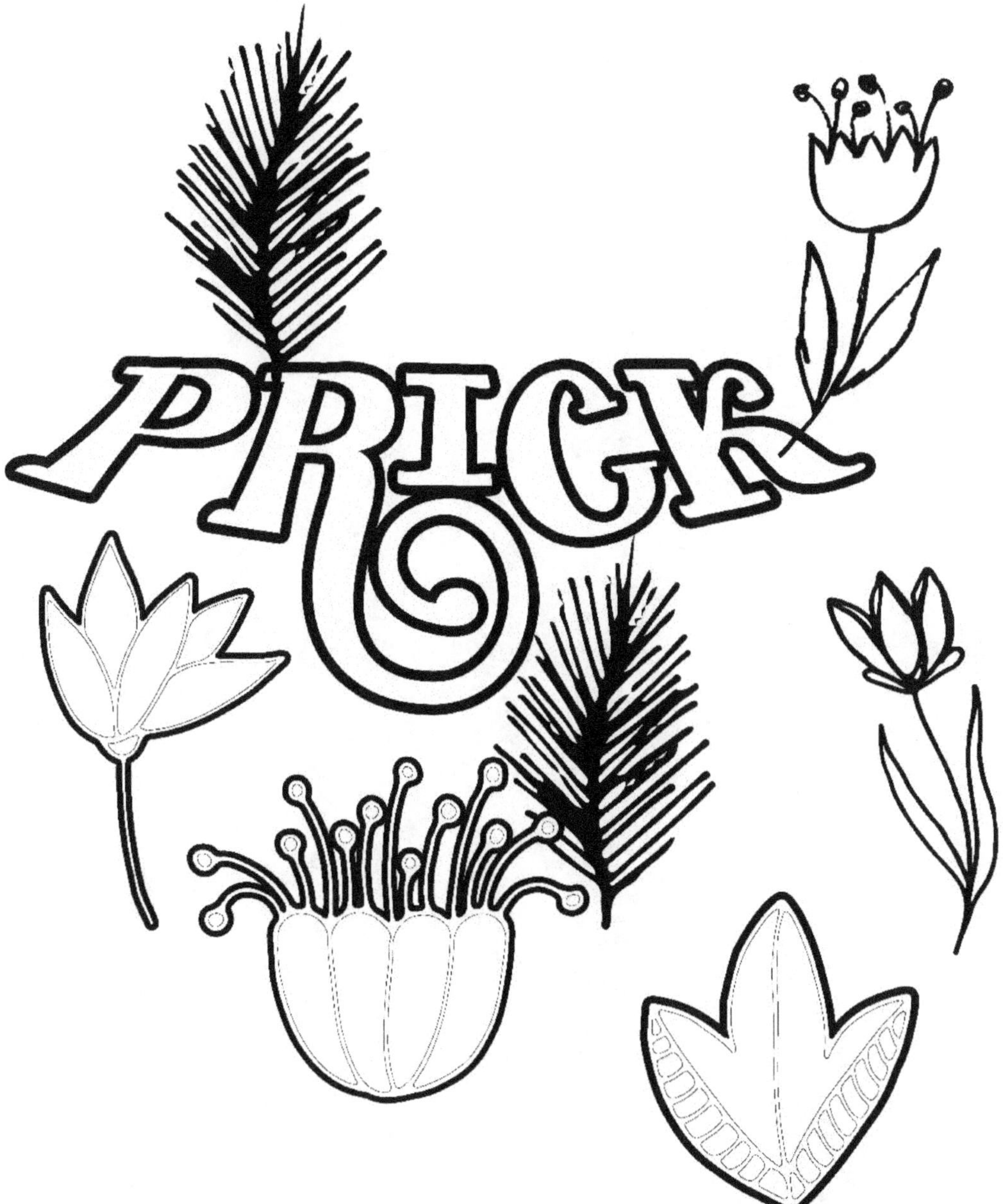
PRICK

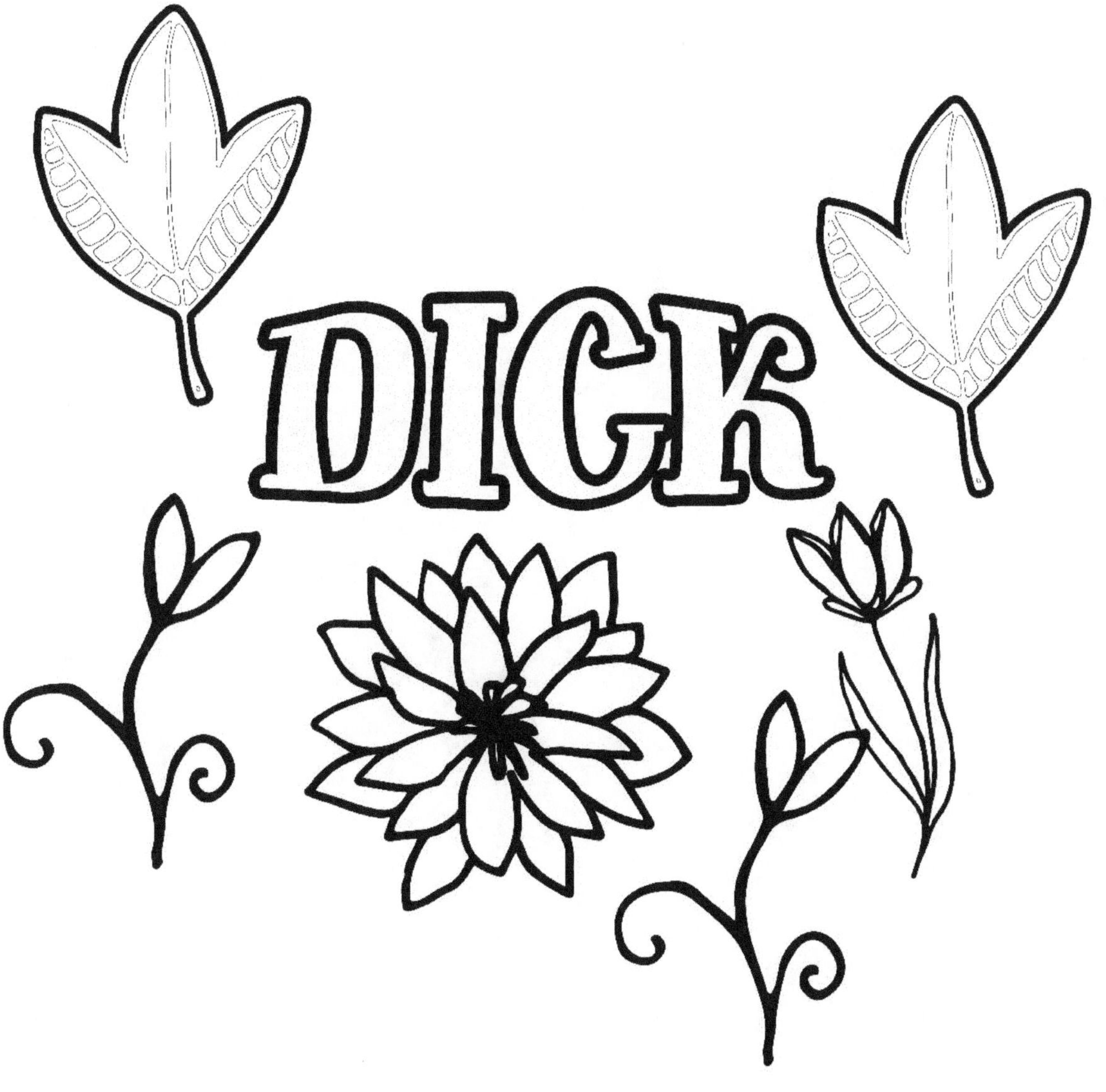
DICK

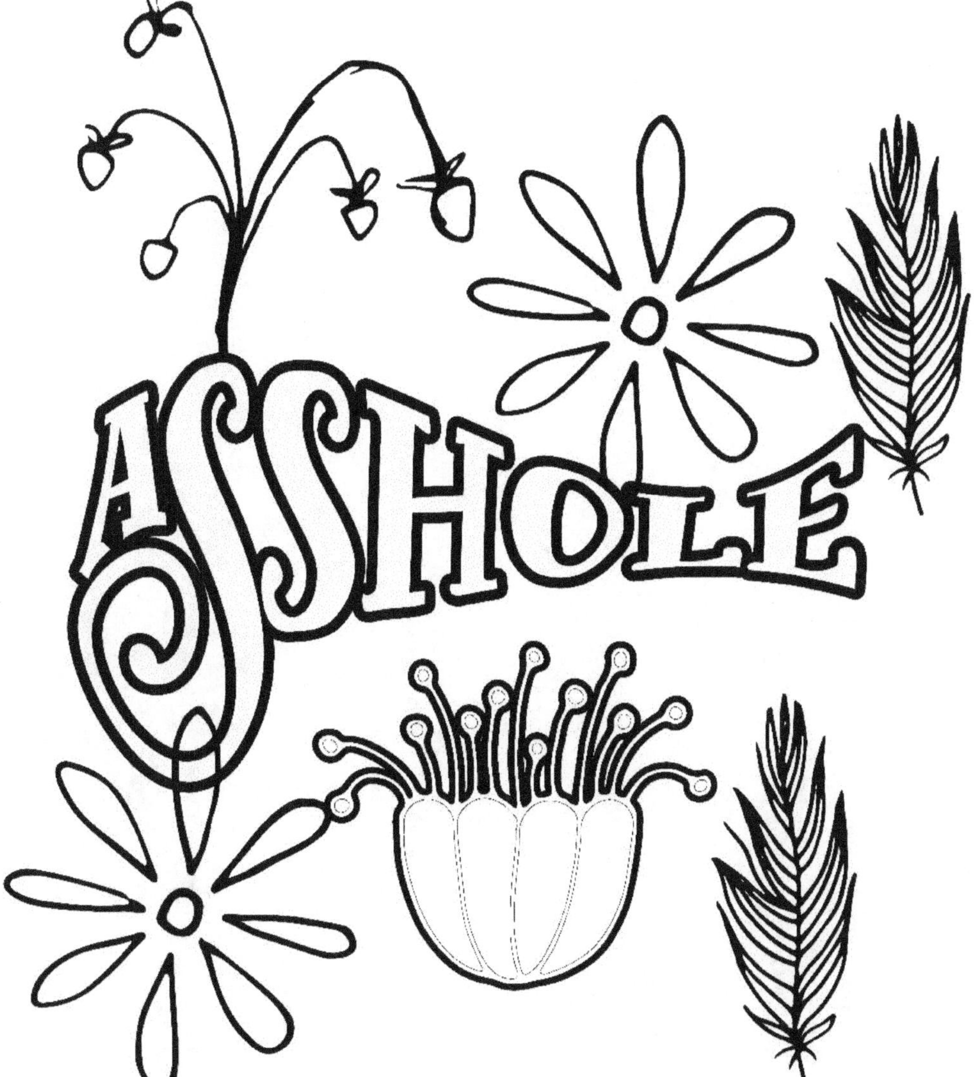
ASSHOLE

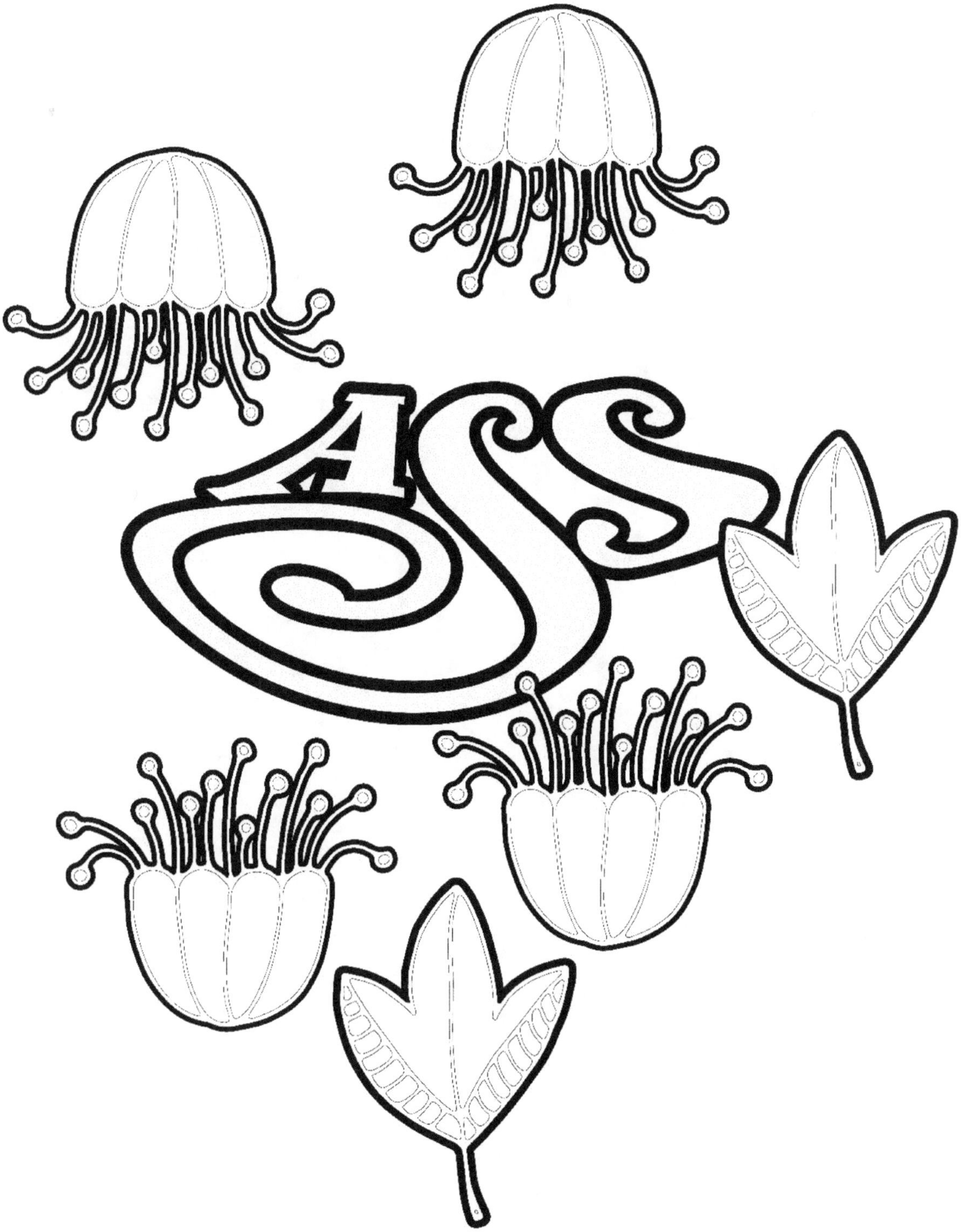
ASS

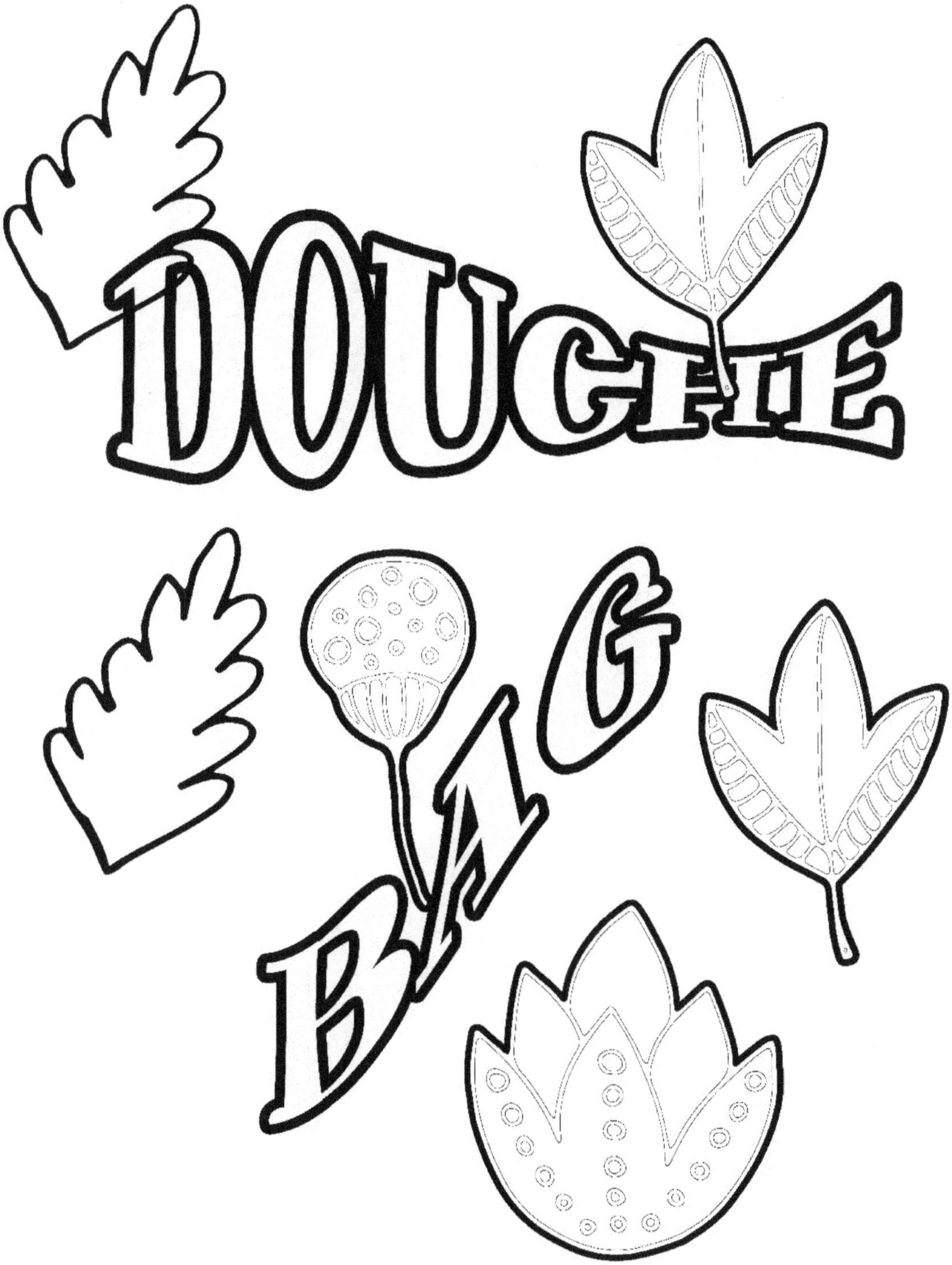
DOUCHE
BAG

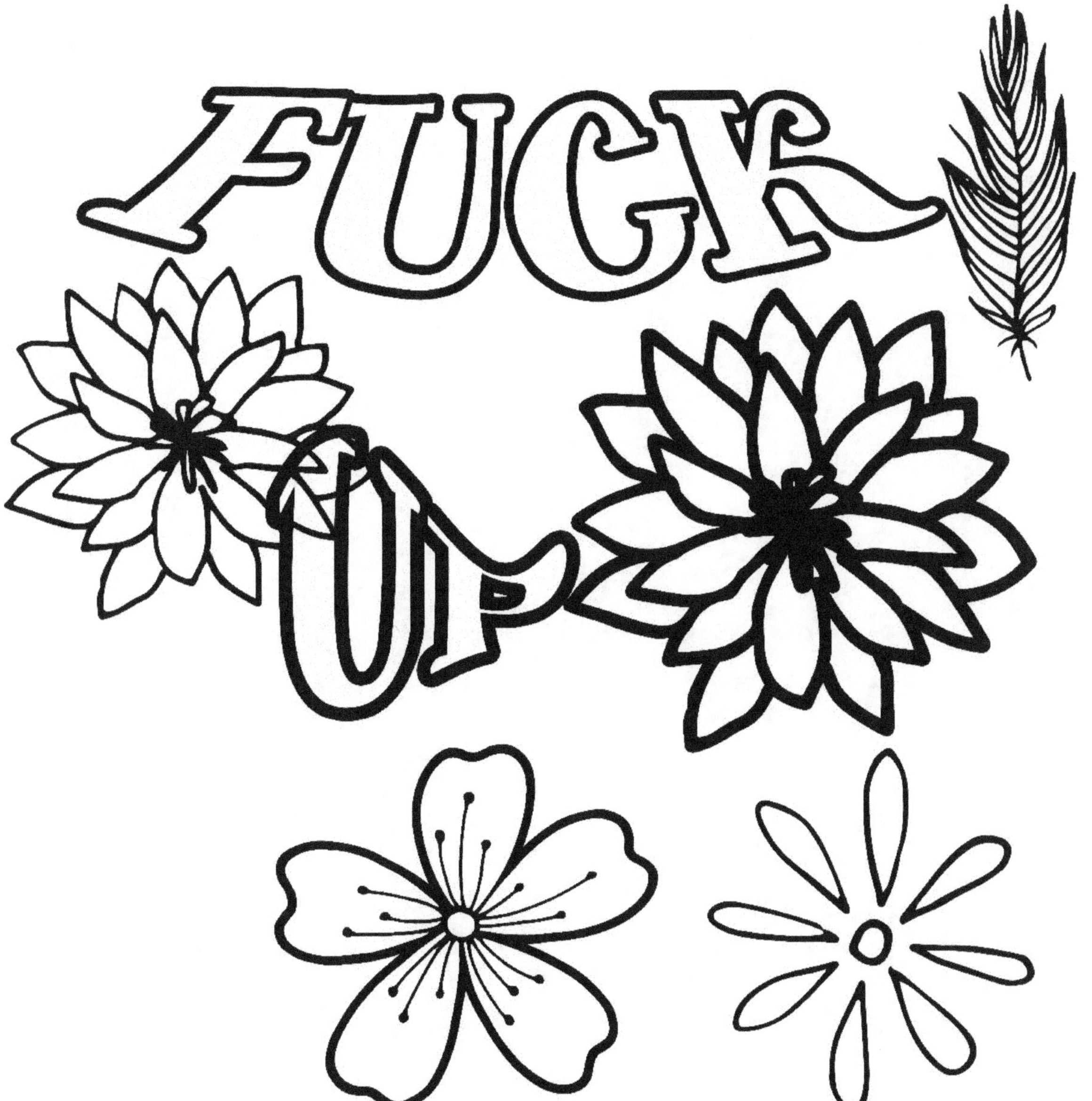
FUCK
UP

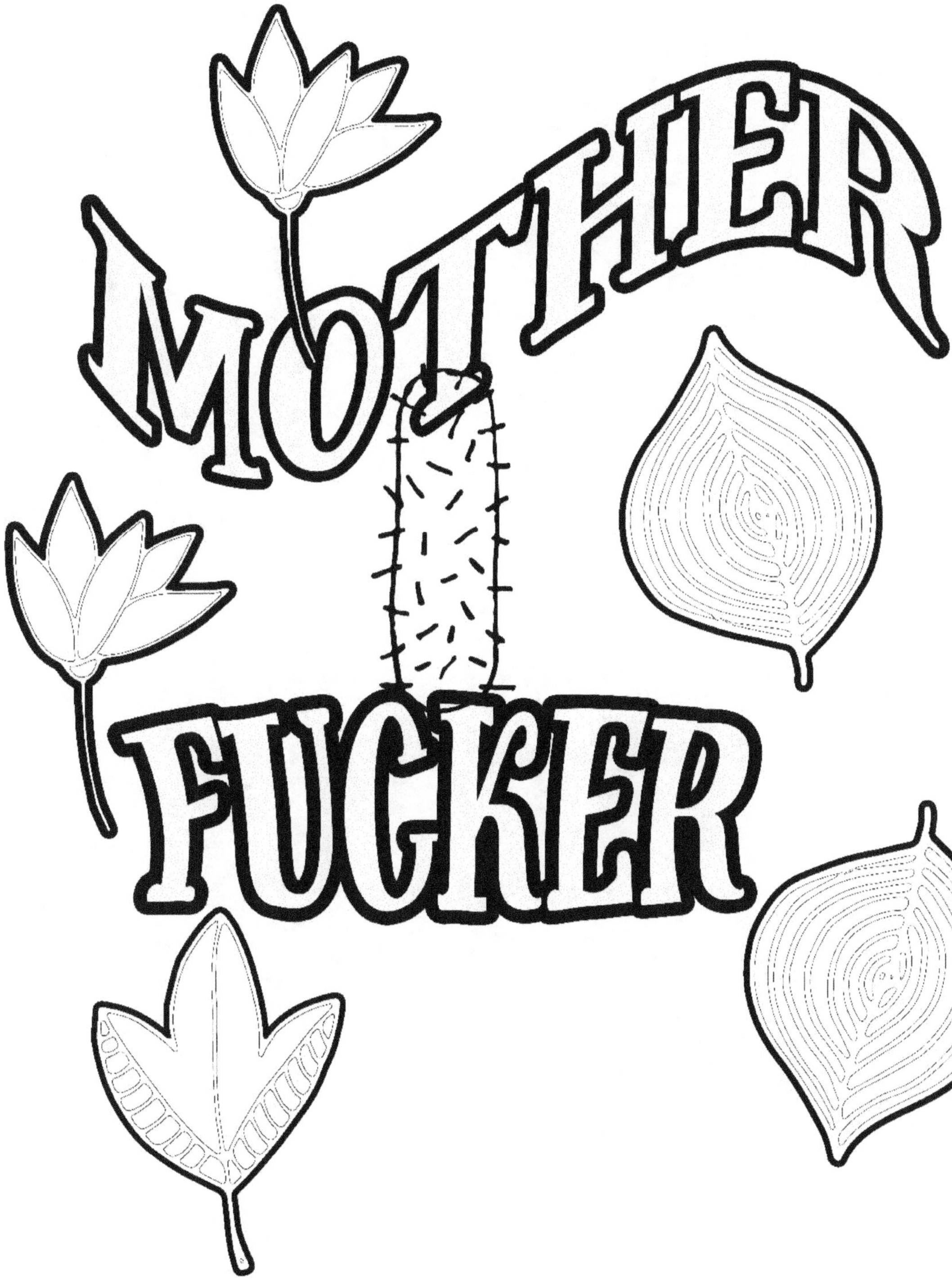
MOTHER
FUCKER

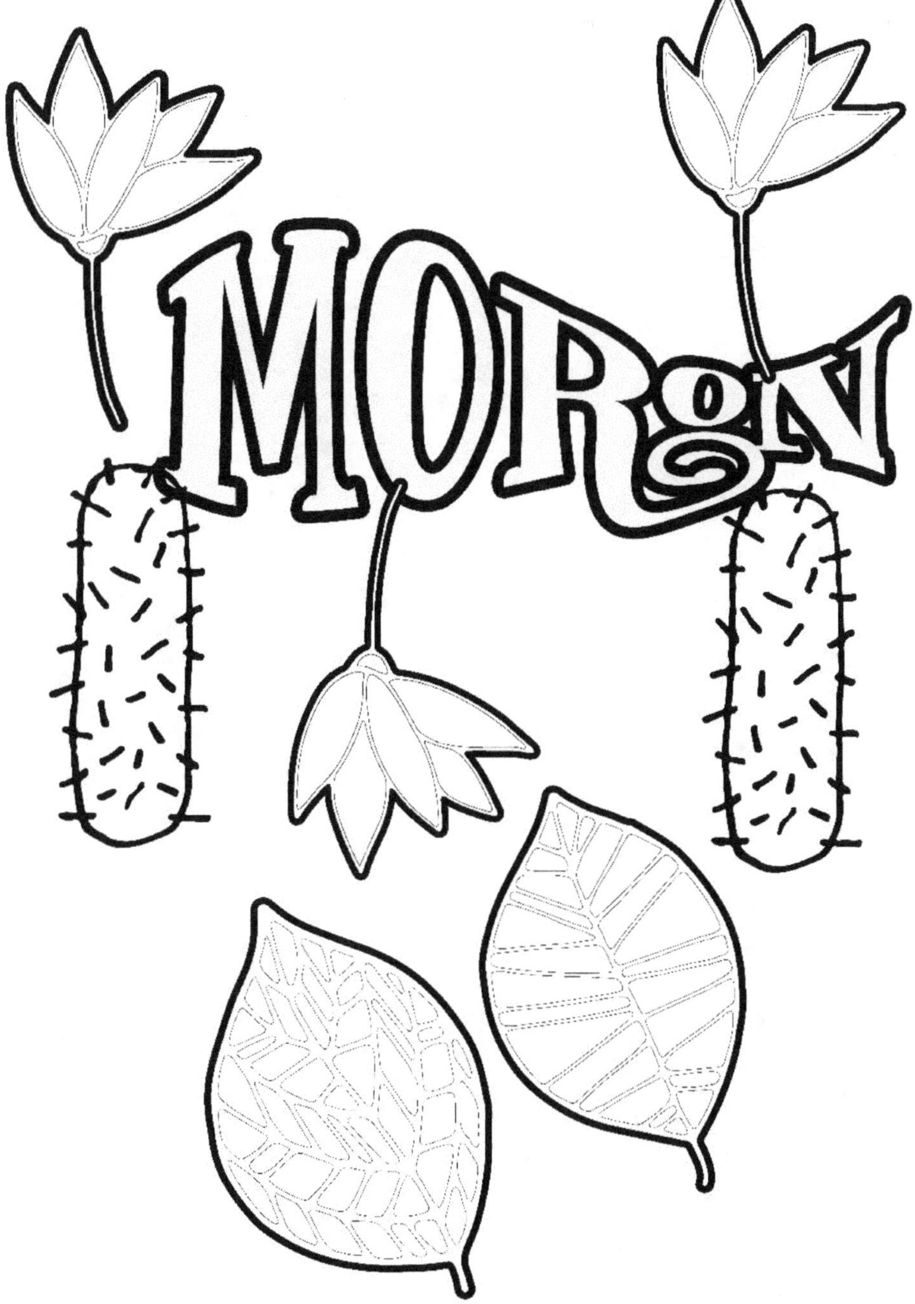
MORgN

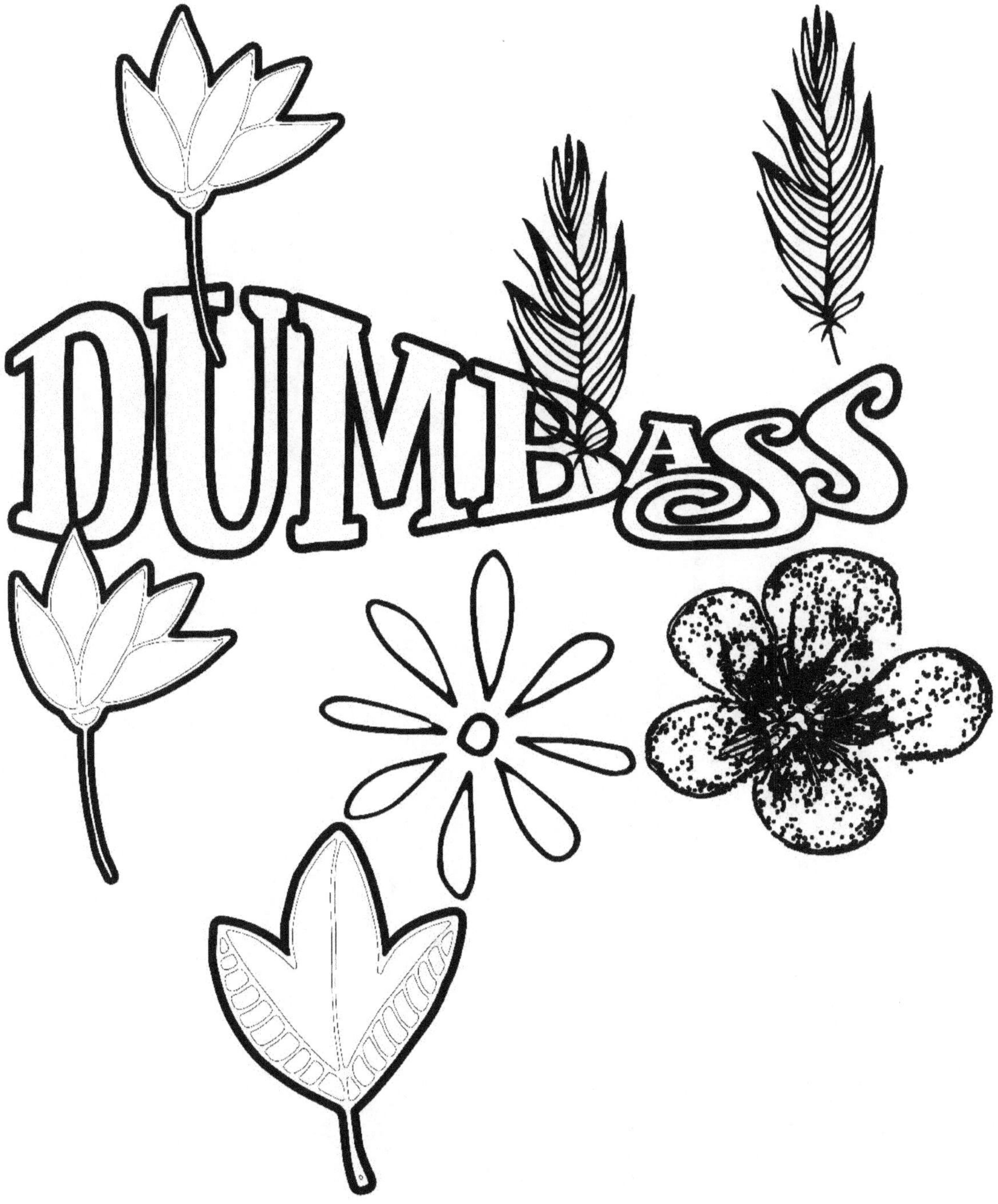
DUMBASS

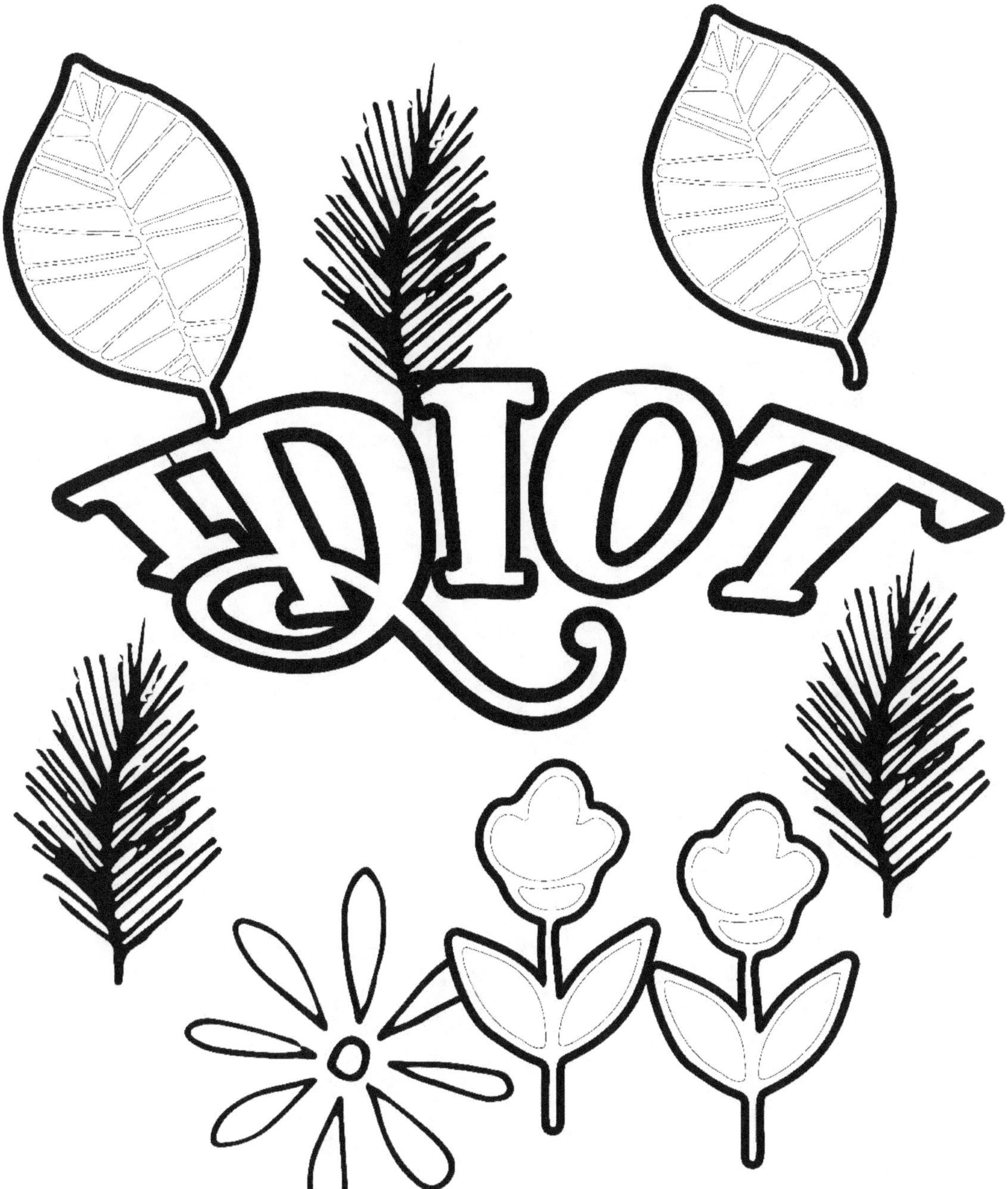
IDIOT

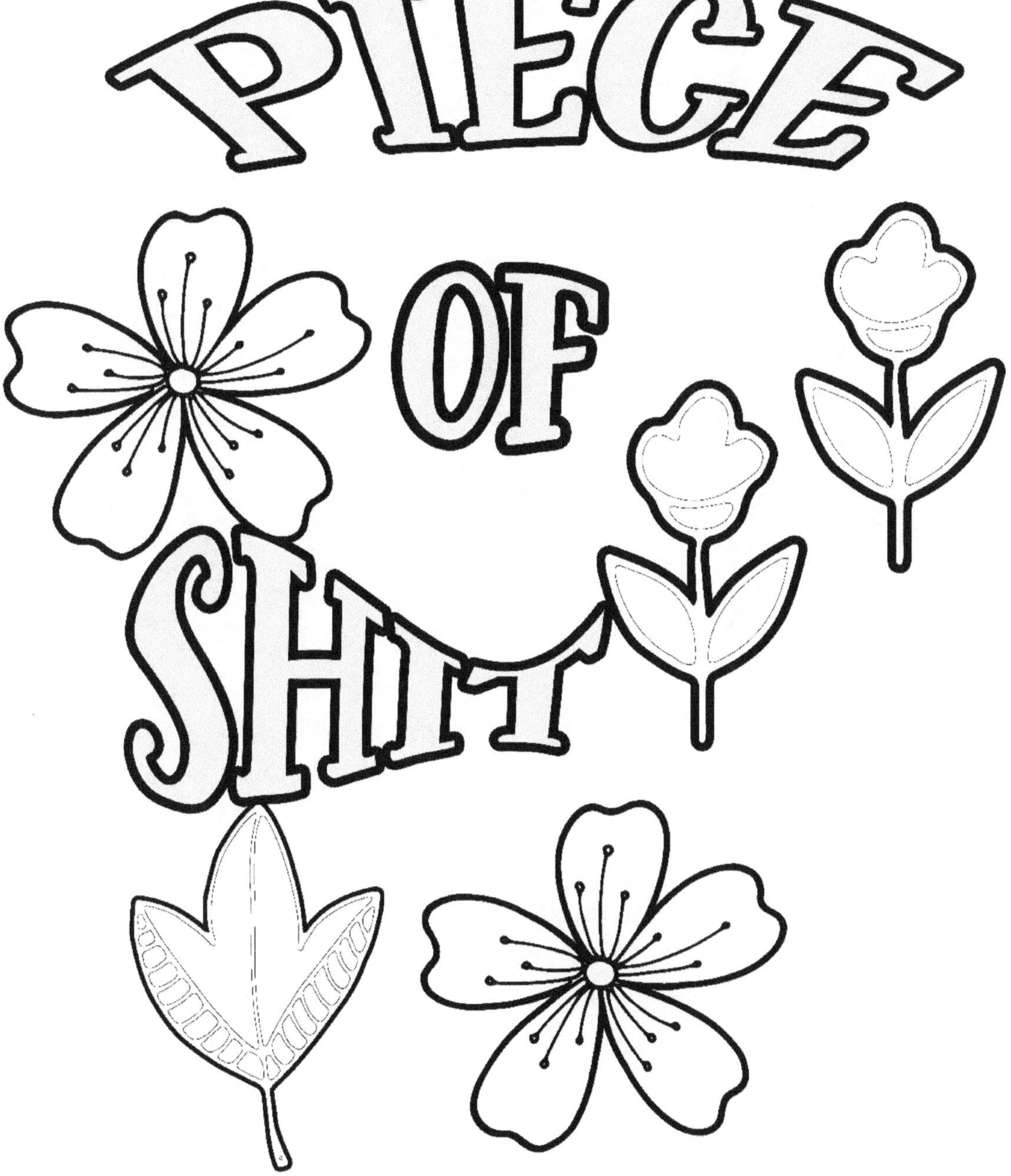
PIECE
OF
SHIT

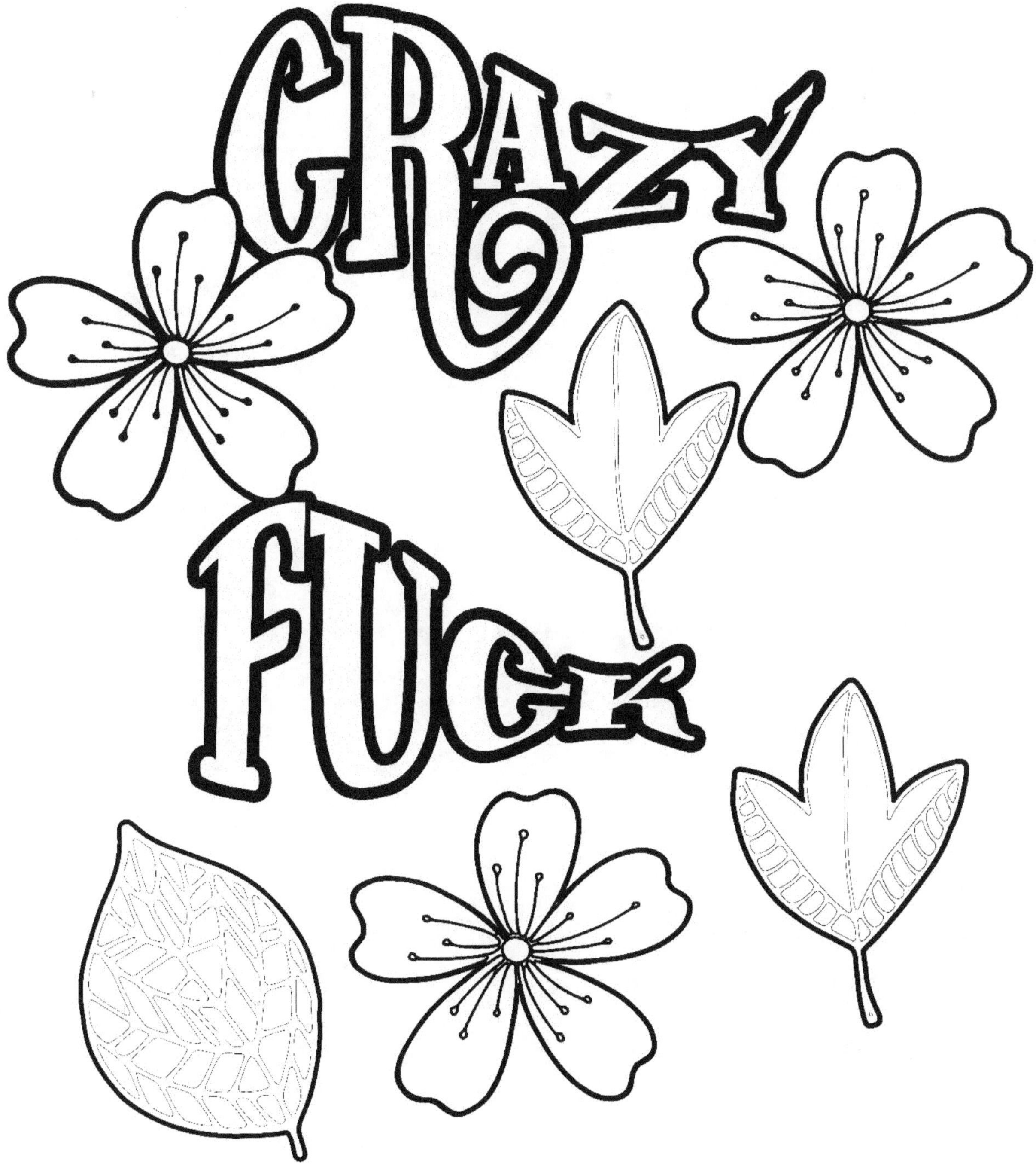
CRAZY
FUCK

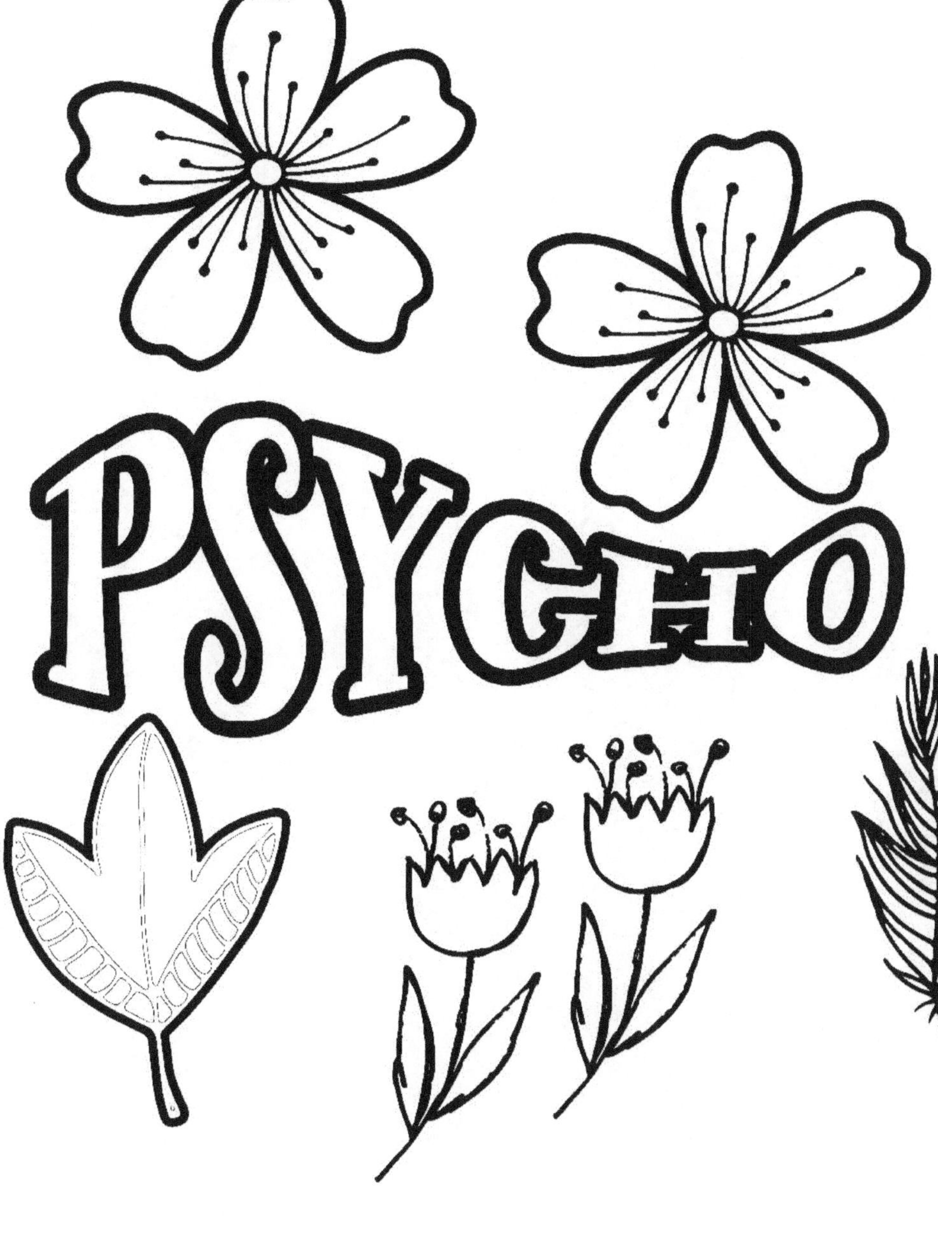
PSYCHO

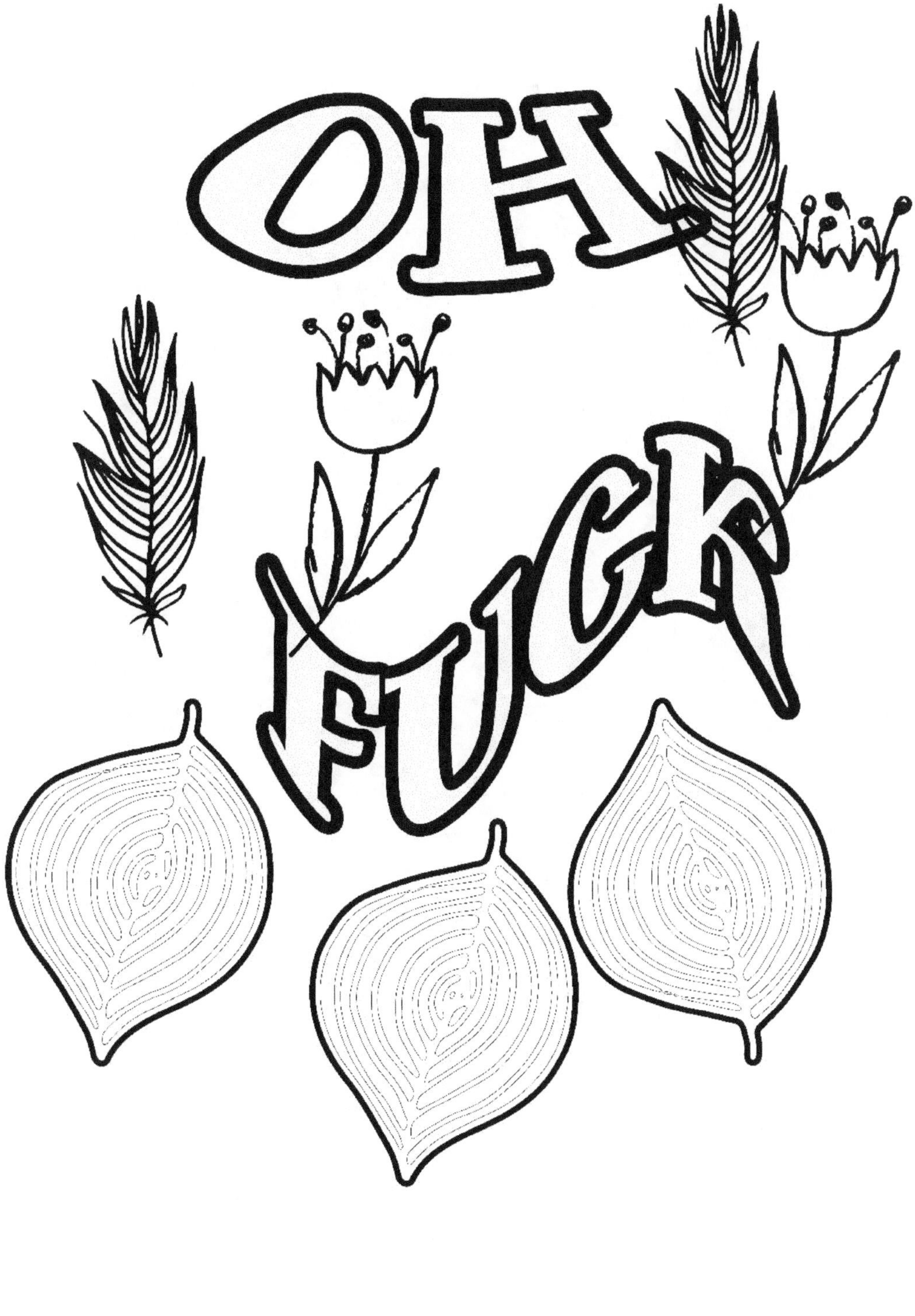
OH
FUCK

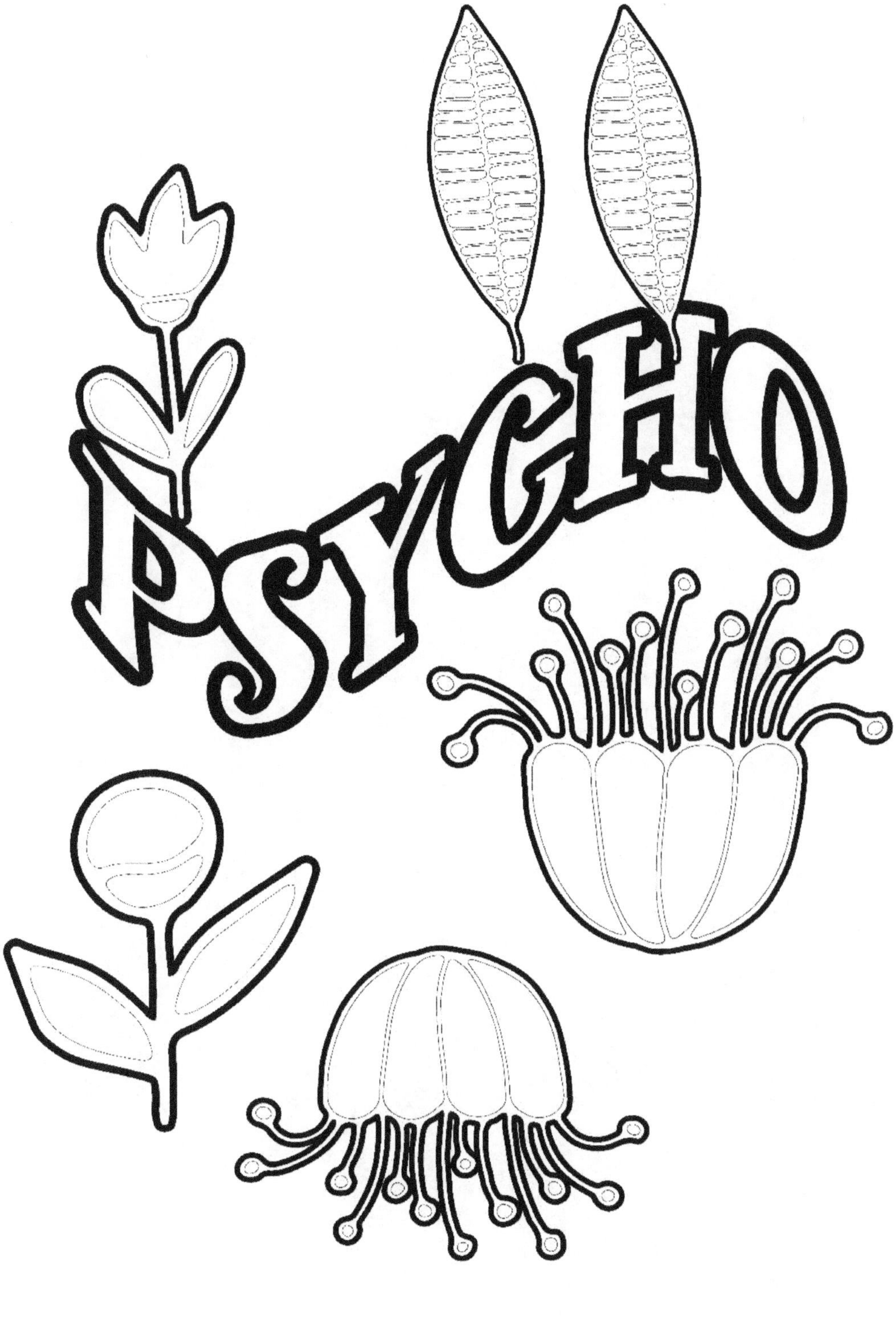
PSYCHO

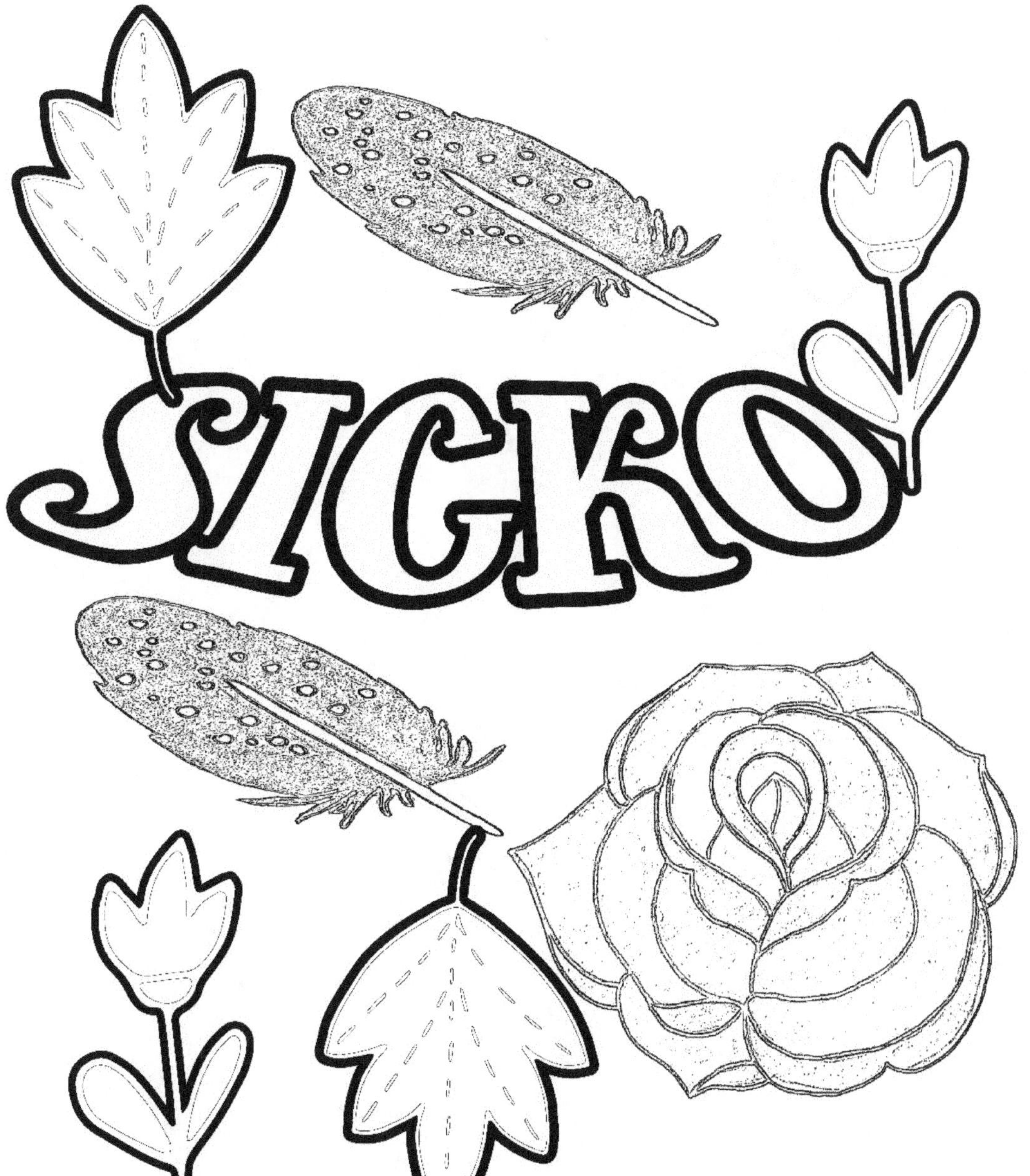
SICKO

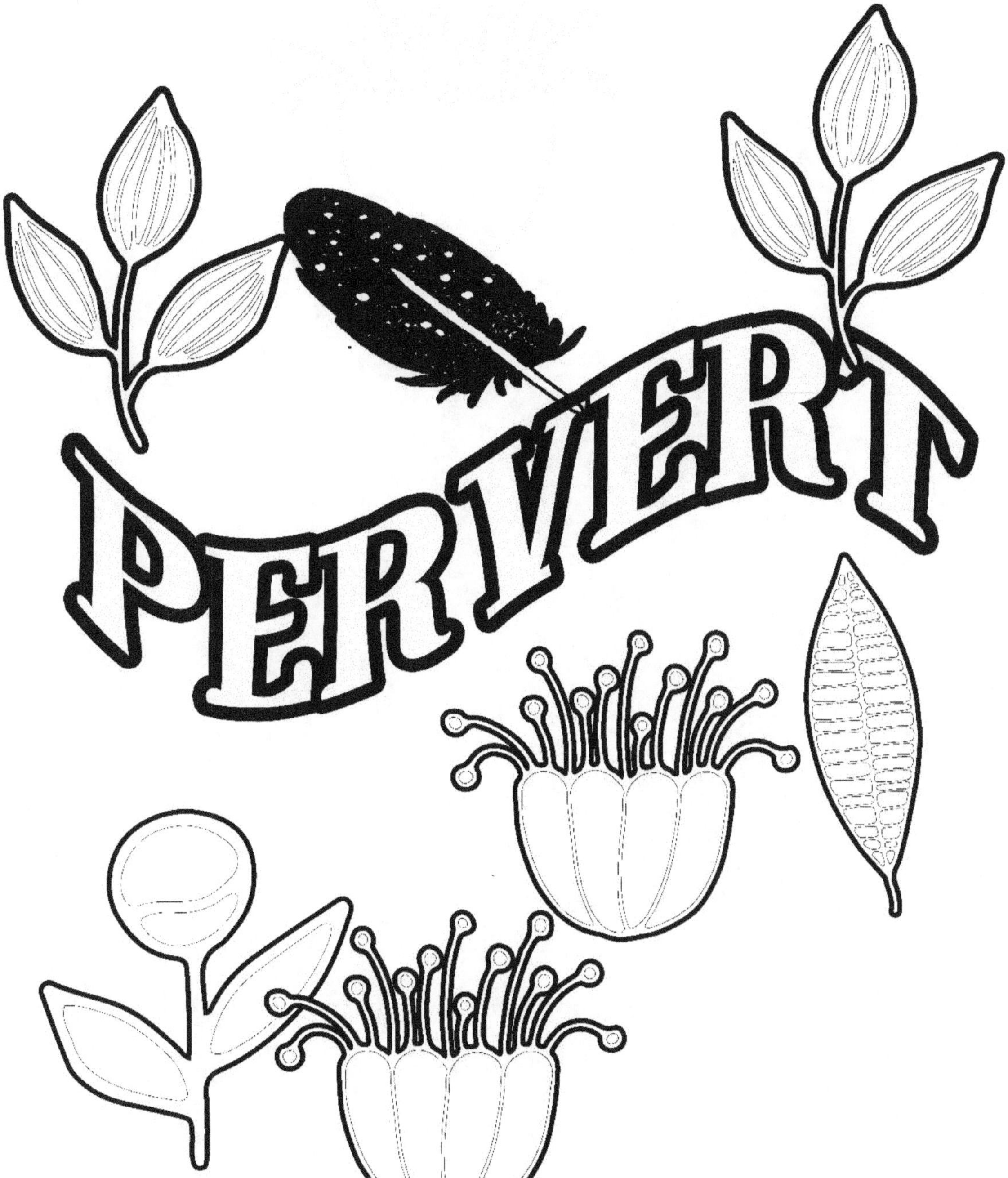
PERVERT

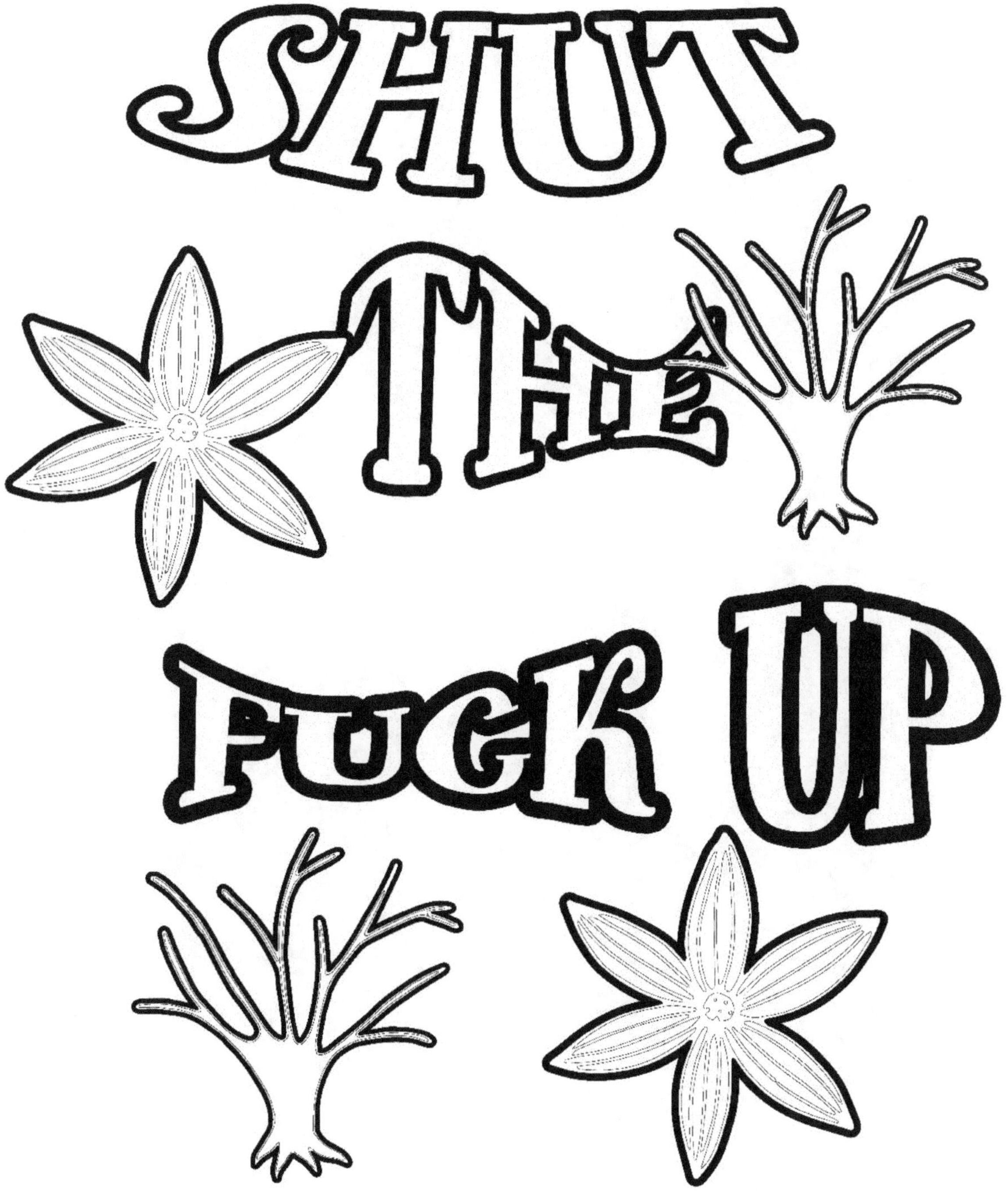
SHUT
THE
FUCK UP

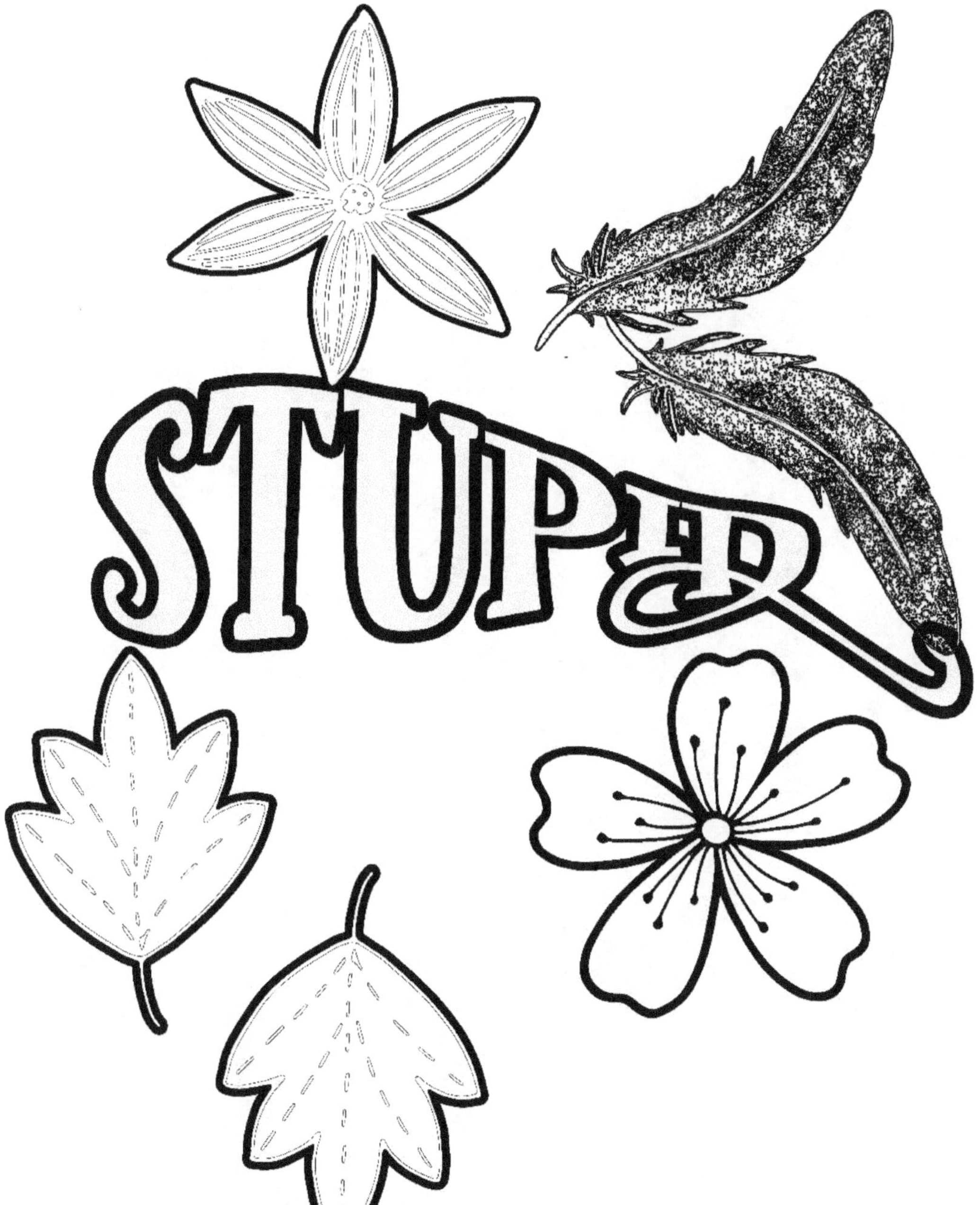
STUPID

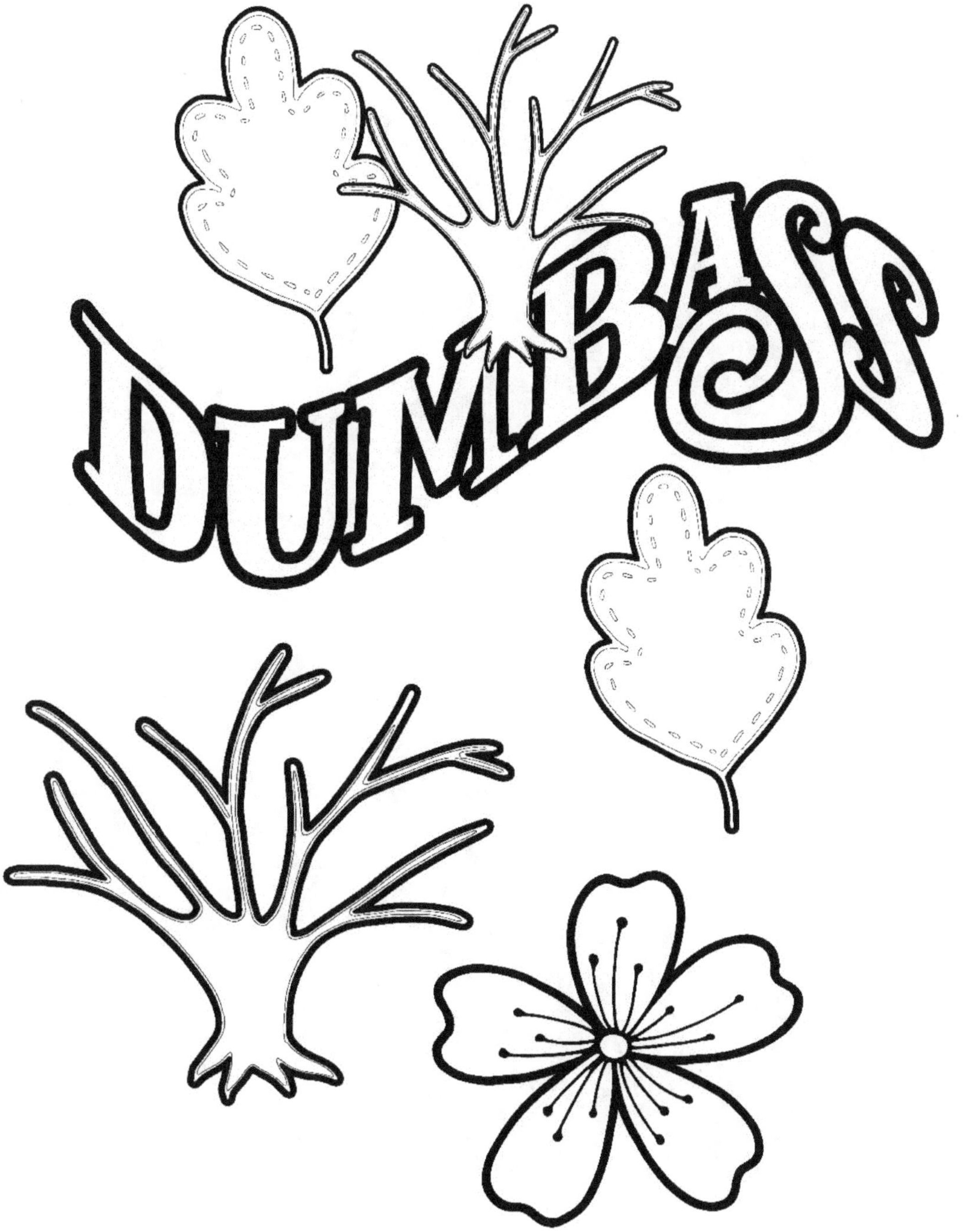
DUMBASS

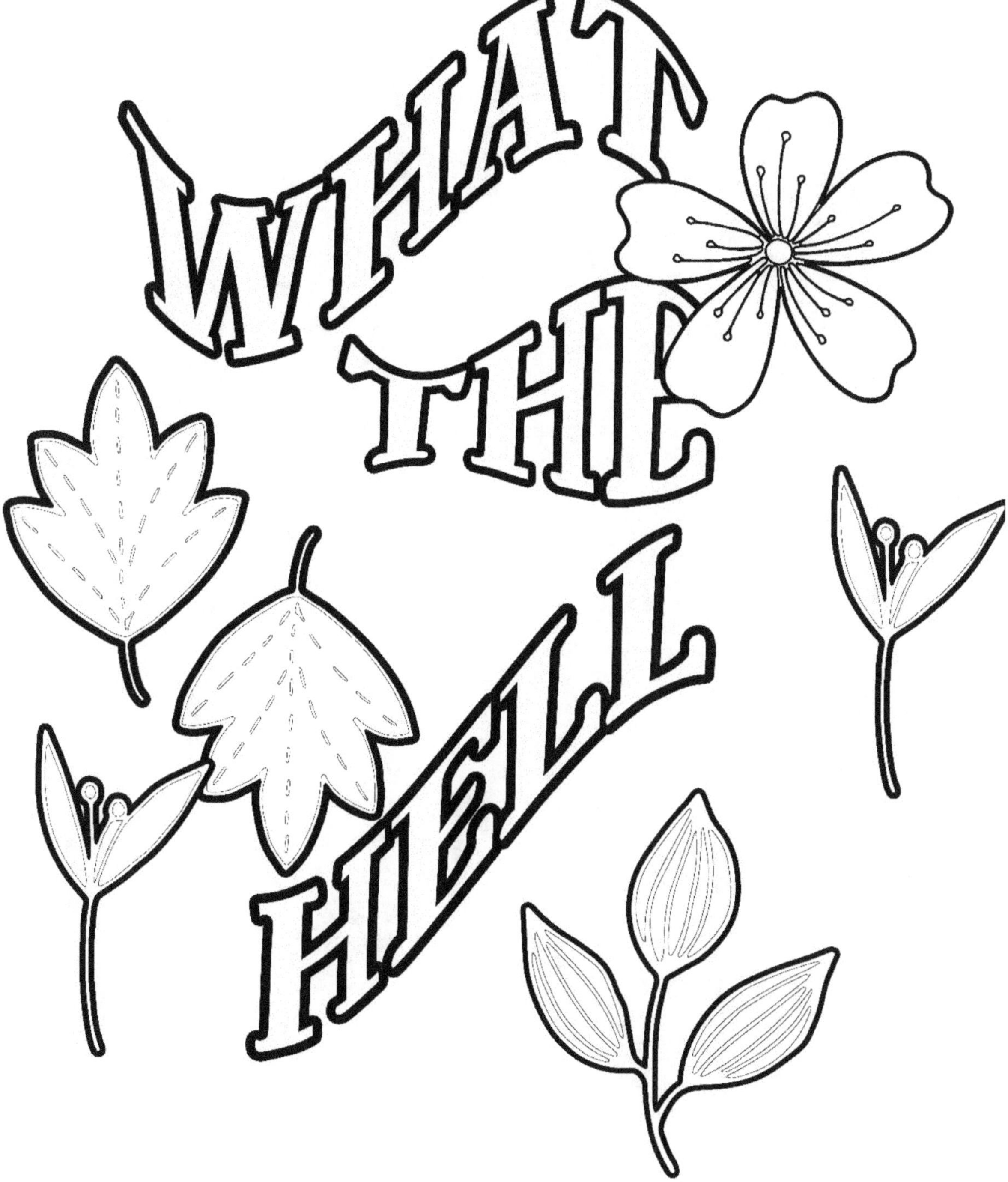
WHAT
THE
HELL

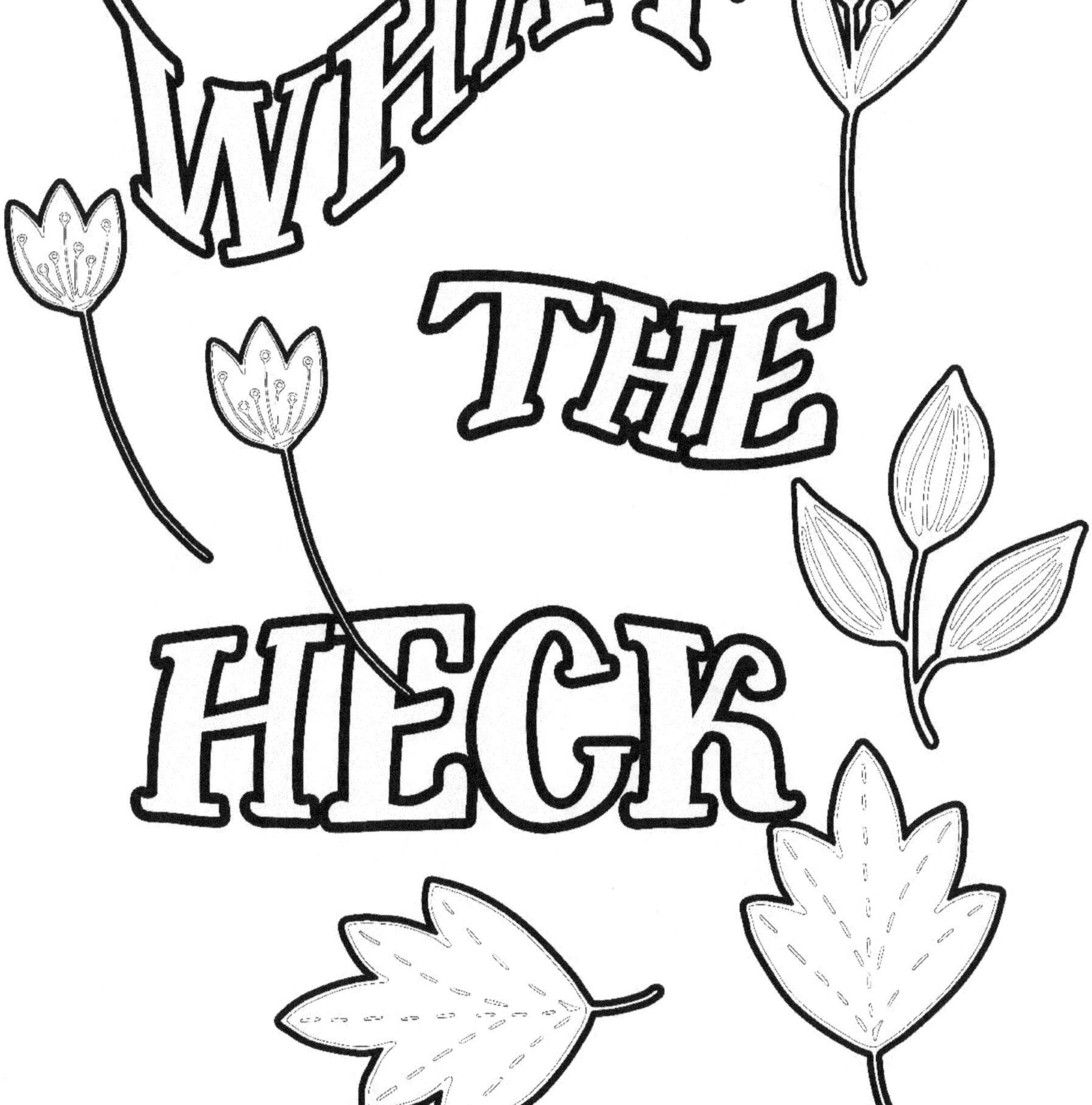
WHAT
THE
HECK

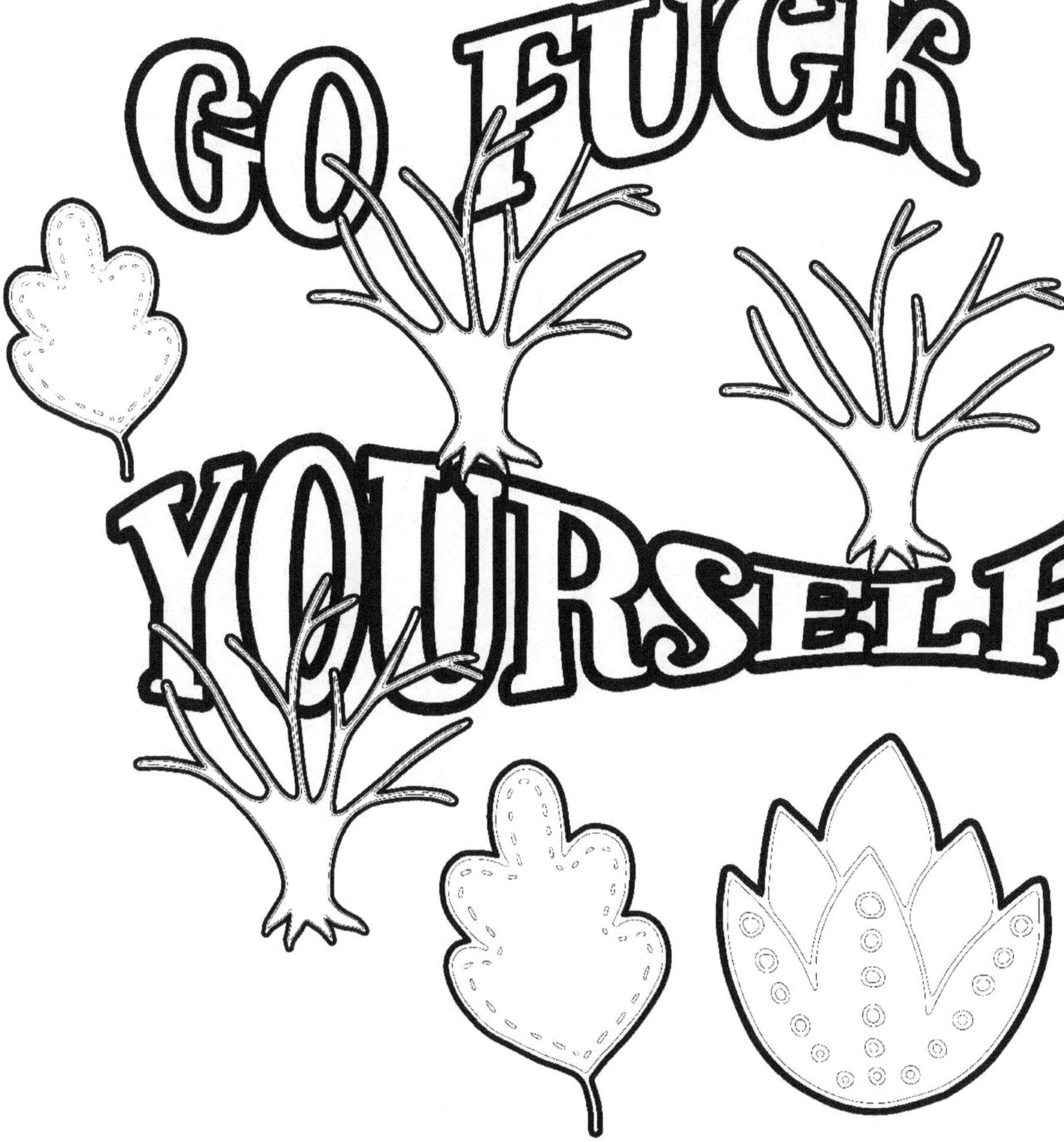
GO FUCK
YOURSELF

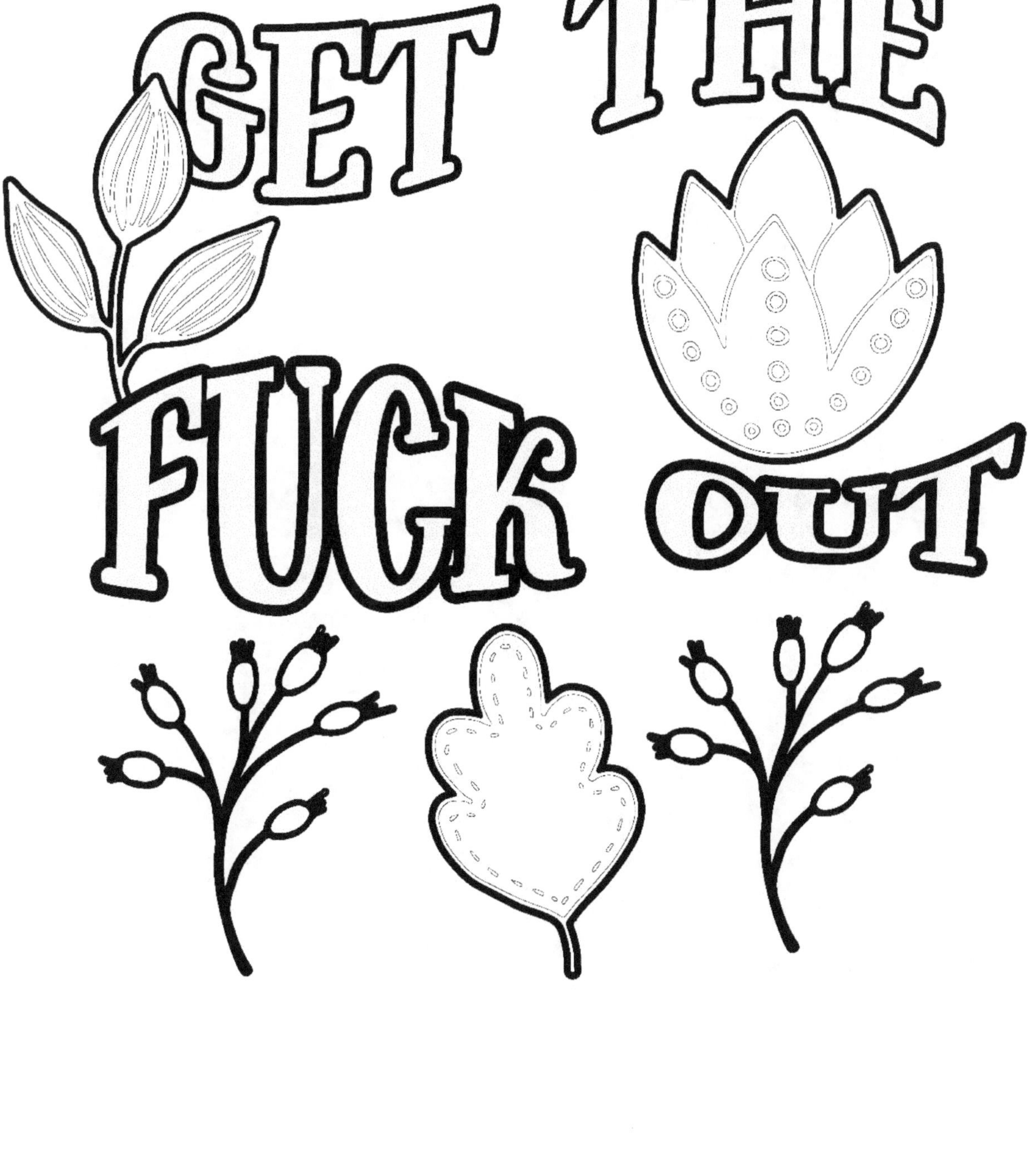
GET THE
FUCK OUT

Note

www.ingramcontent.com/pod-product-compliance
Lightning Source LLC
Chambersburg PA
CBHW080638190526
45169CB00009B/3427
* 9 7 8 1 5 3 3 5 2 1 0 2 6 *